SWERVE

First Edition
ISBN: 978-1-963110-24-1

Published by
Pine Row Press
www.pinerow.com

For permissions or inquiries, please contact:
Pine Row Press
Ft Mitchell, KY
contact@pinerow.com

Swerve

TRACEY KNAPP

Pine Row Press
Ft Mitchell, KY

For my father

Table of Contents

I.

II.

III.

"When you're reaching for a star, there's a long way to fall."

—Steve Martin

I.

Open Mic at Tony's Bar and Grill

There's a man with the rope of a cowbell curled
around his Captain Morgan. He whispers his poems
from a stack of papers, sees your own and nods,
buys you a drink. No conversation needed.
Another person adjusts their blonde wig and quietly
sings *Mi mi mi mi meeeee* repetitively. You wonder
what song they'll actually sing—their wig slightly tilted.
A man cradles his ukulele like a baby. Everyone stares
into their drinks, performing their rehearsal, rubs
the dark worn wood of the bar. You doodle stars
on your pages. Half the people here will only show up
once. No one will tip, and then they'll leave their empties
on the sticky tables, their printouts of songs and poems
on the floor. You were the first to arrive, not thinking
to stop home and put on something more formal
than yoga pants. It doesn't matter. There is some
common urge to say whatever you don't have
anyone to tell except these strangers. It's Sunday night
and raining. Why sit alone silently on your broken couch
with the endless drone of 60 Minutes on the television,
the single-serving life of pasta and tomato sauce, the rain
driving the ants into your kitchen? Someone taps
the microphone, says *HELLO, HELLO.* The wig rises
to the stage, sings "I Fall to Pieces," unconvincingly.

Weather Report with Turkeys

The neighborhood turkey has two girlfriends. They triple shuffle
across the street and my old dog does not know what to think so
he just howls at them through the rain. I slept with my ex
on New Years' Eve while his girlfriend was upstairs.
She didn't mind. They have an arrangement. We both like him
despite his politics. Once, we were the three birds at a funeral
when our hearts were large with loss and love made sense.
It's a strange time to be single. I sleep alone in a converted garage
and dream about floating down a river with a man who has marbled eyes.
My dog wakes me at two in the morning to go outside. I go outside,
and still, I'm single. I love some of my books, their passionate farewells.
I doubt that kind of love will find me. I love the rain and hate it, too,
which must mean it's true love. I refuse to see my doctor because
I don't love my body. I let bad health become a part
of my attitude. I learned to love the mess I made of my thirties.
I love the life that comes back to my dog when he sees
the turkeys meander down the wet road. I need them. I need
people. I need to be alone. I need a nap during a downpour.
Everybody, stop. Close your eyes for a minute. Don't believe
that no one else cares if you're okay. You're totally wrong.
I'm telling you this because I love you.

A Working List

1. ~~Tell your online boyfriend your real age.~~
2. ~~Sweep the seeds and leaves from the porch. The winds were harsh last week.~~
3. Practice sneezing more quietly. Stop the throat-scratch hacking. Who could sleep next to that?
4. ~~Why are you still single? Ask your friends. They know everything about your failures.~~
5. Dump your shitty friends who can detail your failures verbatim back to you.
6. Do the dishes. Remove your socks from the bed sheets.
7. ~~Bobby pins are not Q-Tips. Baby wipes are not bathtubs.~~
8. ~~Commit to eating like a person. With other people. Stop wasting your money on wine and prepackaged food at the 7-Eleven.~~
9. Spend more time talking to yourself outdoors at night when stoned.
10. ~~Stop drinking wine. Stop drinking. But only when alone. Except if you were drinking with people beforehand, and you came home to your dog.~~
11. ~~Watch less TV. Except, re-watch the movie, Frances Ha. You are a dancer, and you have dreams.~~
12. All those goddamn books you buy and barely open.
13. Make the world more beautiful! Take one earring, preferably dangled and missing its mate. Hang it from an old nail or forgotten hook. A quiet, lucky place.
14. ~~Quit losing earrings. Quit earrings. Quit things.~~
15. ~~Put your old jeans in a box and then the attic. And someday when you move into a new bright house with a new love, you'll pull them out, thin and mothy, you'll delight: I CAN'T BELIEVE IT! THEY ALMOST FIT!~~
16. ~~Grow things. Give away things. Give away your neighbor's excessive lemons. Your tight jeans.~~
17. ~~Recycle more. Stop hoarding the little gifts that someone gives you when they kind of liked you because they~~

~~barely knew you. The broken ceramic rabbit isn't even emblematic.~~

18. Appreciate your one good knee, your moisturized cuticles, and the hair that grew back on your head after you got rid of that fucking IUD.
19. ~~Reach into that folder of old letters pull out the one with the nicest paper. Don't read it. Just touch it and let it be the cramp in the gut of all the people who used to love you by hand.~~
20. Celebrate your old man-dog. In the following order, give him: a walk, a scratch, a bath, a treat, a nap, a brush, a walk, a treat, a nap.
21. Write down a list of what you could do to be your best.
22. Narrow it down to ten.

Answer the Question

Did you ever ask your mother what a lover was?
Why her eyes turned black when she smoked
over the sink? Did your brother tell you why
he shot his finger, or burned a hole in his plastic
clock? Did your father show you how to load
the ornamental bullets from the belt of his
officers' gun? Why did you smash slate with a hammer?
Can you name your scars and their reasons? Why
would you nail your dolls to trees? Why did you stop
tap dancing? Where were you when Jack and Jennifer
first kissed on Days of Our Lives? Skittles or Starburst?
Pick one. What about the first time a bee stung your ankle
in an old tire? Or falling off the picnic table:
do you just recall the story of it, or the fierce pinch
of stitches on your head? Was the hose left on to flood
the small lilies or water the salamanders under the old wheel?
You forgot your first doll's name: true or false.
Yes or no: the window to the roof was a portal to the stars.
Did you see many shooting stars? Yes. Many, many
shooting stars. Lovers, yes, light years later.

How I Will Do It

Under the glint of your glasses I will love you

as the last can of Sprite sizzles in your hand

I will drink your extra Sprite and I will walk your dog I will

love you under the yellow basement lights of the DMV

I will let you feed me foreign candies in the taxi to the airport

and on the plane I will give you the window I will let you

hold the Skymall and someday we'll buy the lap pool darling someday

the smallest book lamp you'll ever need I will never read Better Homes

& Gardens I promise you I will never let the literature of housewives

bring us down even with an apron or a minivan I will

still spank you gently and always tell you love you when

you are walking towards the door I never love you more than then

Wish Control

There is a woman digging through
her purse, dumping it out on the bench
at the bus stop and she needs something
now, and I don't know what, but it's urgent.
My dog insists we stop at the next tree,
and then the next, smells a specific scent—
skunk urine he wants to take along
on our walk—so I drag him from patch
to patch and we investigate the abandoned
sneakers on the sidewalk that wish for feet.
We keep moving, past a window filled with yellow
shirts perfect for spring, and my wallet sings from
inside my purse. I cringe when I see the same man
at the 7-Eleven trade his scratch-off lotto
tickets for a new set, wonder how the cycle
will persist—more scratch-offs, more small joys
surrendered again and again.
My neighbor sold the home he dreamed
of dying in. He brings the boxes
to the dump, filled with years of frames
and figurines he kept for the family
that never quite worked out the way
he'd wished for: a wife departed, a broken
son—and I take his old Theremin, plug it in
and wave my hands around its antenna,
make a wavering moan that starts a cry from
the cat outside, a cemetery sound, a summoning.

To the Sea

My mother took the bag from its box—
home to my father's ashes for thirteen years—
and poured its heft into a form she made

on the potter's wheel—damp and unfired.
She pinched the rotating lip, sealed the clay
perfectly shut, a technique I haven't yet mastered.

We planned to launch it like a football at low tide,
but when we arrived, the beach was lined with people;
there was no subtle way for me to toss it out past
the children kneeling in the surf, the surfers awaiting the break.

To carry my father out with one hand, arm above my head,
heavy with him—or hold him against my chest, side-stroking
with one hand while the clay disintegrated into the water—
I wasn't dressed for it.

Instead, we dropped him in the water by the docks
by the old Shrimp Shack, all 6'4" of him,
and I watched the vessel slowly descend, a few bubbles
emerging like the last breath from a dying lung.

The Obvious Cracks

Every night, my father sat there
with his Schafer Light and sci-fi paperback,
mustachioed, content and probably
farting while the news buzzed on the TV.
He could hear just fine but liked it loud.

I kept that beast of an armchair,
despite the stains and cat-scratched back.
To have it, a difficult joy.

Homegrown

barefoot footbridge riverrock minnow

horsepuck stonewall mosspaint wallpaper

shadowlurk mudsling brownblack headwrap

stonethrow turkeyduck hedgehog middlebrook

creekrot bug tent handsaw brow sweat

motionsick chinstrap kickstand handsfree

prickerbush backyard forest mapletree

Dunlap tireswing roperot doubleknot

eyecrud milquetoast tearduct knockknee

lightening bug backhill river road sundown

flashlight window starshower rooftop

Note: *"Homegrown" is written after "Silent Poem" by Robert Francis.*

Gorilla,

it has been a stressful week. Gorilla,
I do not want to transcribe meeting notes.
I want only soft foods. My jaw hurts when
I chew, goddamn gorilla.

A stranger overheard a conversation
with my brother about insomnia and she told me
I should eat more bananas. I hate bananas.
I hate lying in bed for five hours awake
but bananas are not worth it. I suck at gorilla.

When I was a child, I had a recurring nightmare
about you. Sometimes my family would escape
from your gorilla barn by wading through quicksand
to our car and then speed away.

I can also remember your frustration:
a little blue Toyota shredding the dirt
road into dust like nobody's gorilla.

Gorilla, I could climb into your museum
skin and drag my knuckles, show all my teeth
in a power move, but instead,
after I take a deep inhale, I exhale gorilla.

In moments of heavy traffic, I have learned
how to count my breath as
three gorillas in, three gorillas out:

Gorilla, gorilla, gorilla.

Apology

I punctured the gauzy nest open with a crow feather,
letting the feet of twenty caterpillars dazzle
my hand, over my wrist. I wanted to be a part of it—

nature, I guess—so it only made sense to take them
home in a large jar filled with broken twigs and grass.
I hovered my hands around the glass, watched

their bodies crawl and fall. It was a cruel act,
to wreck their woven home, steal their bodies.
I tried to be tender, though; I stroked the soft

fur on their small, long forms. and I never meant
to kill a single one. I was seven then. Didn't know
the caterpillar mind, didn't know what one

might need in a home besides Apple Jacks,
my parents' bed to crawl into at night.
So when the sun released the morning

upon the jar in my window, I forgot it. You know
the rest: my mother mad, the toilet flush,
my panicked hands tearing a piece of tissue into dust.

Thirteen

At the campground, I enjoyed the ocean, hot dogs, and flirting
with danger—letting the older teenage boys touch my legs
in the rec hall, wearing a reckless bikini, my new small boobs.

My anxiety rose like a pubescent pimple as my family
slowly became alien to me, their public humiliations
at the McDonalds drive-thru, a unanimous silence over
fast food fish strips and the evening news.

In Shop Rite, my mother paid for the pot roast with
a paper check—her elegant penmanship and halter top
seducing the checkout clerk while I pocketed
two packs of Juicy Fruit.

I locked my bedroom door and lay in my bed with four pieces
of gum in my mouth and a pillow up my nightgown.
I found comfort in that pregnancy while my old blonde dolls
languished in a broken bassinet. Thirteen is no age
to be a woman, with the fits of tears and unfamiliar bleeding.

At the end of summer, I raked a path through the woods,
sorted stones into rectangular beds. I liked to think
that was as much a home as the house up the hill,
clearing those loam floors, leaning fallen branches into quiet huts.

I wrote my name in the dirt with a stick. I nursed a chipmunk back
from my cat's attack, stroked his striped bitten mass. I collected
salamanders from beneath an old wagon wheel— their cold
bodies, their simple, dark lives. My own life,
still simple, just beginning to darken.

Swerve

The moment you realize
          your life is over halfway over,
                    another car clips your bumper
          on the bridge, nudging you into the breakdown
lane, and yes! This is about
          the right age to ricochet
          off the road towards the edge,
                    a quick flash from the water
          below before you swerve
back into traffic. You tap
          the brakes, make a swift exit
                    towards the next Saturday
          brunch involving oysters
and a mojito mocktail,
          which is a sexy way of saying
                    crushed mint and simple syrup.
          Nothing is simple anymore.
Your knees ache and everyone
          knows it. Everyone talks about
                    adult orthodontics. By now,
          everyone knows death, it's many faces.
Everyone talks about being irregular.
          You don't even flinch anymore
                    when the labs come back
          irregular. Your body atrophies
despite minimal efforts:
          each night you complete three
                    sun salutations in memory of
          your yoga ass. Where is that
oomph that once moved you
          to fit your foot behind your head?
                    Your hips slip. The risks are real.
          Your older brother walks too fast,

which reminds you of the time
you ran the suburban streets
of West Newton, Massachusetts
in a sports bra and soccer shorts,
waving your middle finger around
at any passing car that nearly bumped
you off the road, just make it
to the next block then the next,
desperate for the finish, then
a cigarette and bourbon.

II.

Leaving South of Market

Industrial lamps drench the dancefloor with diffused light.
Glow sticks threading her fingers, a dancer hula-hoops
the room. Here, everything is almost like you remember,

every flash pulsing in time to the beat. The guy you've
been flirting with moves your hand over his pants and you,
too old for this shit, get up and pull your vintage velvet

duster from the floor. At the exit, two big dudes in security
vests wave you outside after one stamps your hand, the ink
fracturing into the lines of your wrist in the rain. Nearby,

someone in a Santa suit flicks a cigarette and soon, the two
of you are laughing while exhaling rings of smoke, *ho, ho, ho*
into the low fog. But you are too old for cigarettes, too old

for Santa. Sausages and peppers marinate the air. 1:13 a.m.
Police shovel tents into a dump truck. Someone's set a heap
of garbage on fire. The fog swallows the smoke, the sound

of rain and fire engines. Ambulances pierce the stoplights
towards the highway onramp. In the cab, your driver
grumbles about crossing the bridge and now you're

calculating distance by the number of exits and freeways,
not footsteps or city blocks. The broken streetlamp outside
your building flashes like disco strobe. You rush to

the bathroom for your first pee in hours, peel your fake
eyelashes into the sink, scrub the glitter from your face.
The small hours of morning open like a sinkhole. The moon

fights for her moment from behind the clouds. A large
mosquito throws itself upon the porch lamp, bumping
against the glass as if it could become the light.

When I'm Cold

When a turkey crosses
a double lane where I live
in California, the cars crowd
the street in the kind of pause
that makes you think
people might read poetry.
When people read poetry,
they slow down for something
like an irregularity, a turkey
darting across a city road.

When I drive through
West Marshfield, Ohio,
I am surrounded by a crossing
of fifty pheasants. It's only a crossing
when there is a conflict
of direction. I pause at the stop sign
and it's dawn, no other cars in sight.
The frost clings to the ground
for its final moments. I exhale
through my mouth
to see my own dense breath
and I'm alone again.

When I'm alone, I huddle with
a fake down pillow.
I like to be cold when I'm alone.
Most solitary people do.
When I am an object,
I am also a subject.
Most women know
how that goes. When my lover
sleeps, I wake and leave the room.

While awake, I sneeze
and huddle on the couch
in the dark. I hold a hot mug
to my face, huff the lemon
and paprika tea that is meant
to clear toxins when you are low.
I am low, but for the strays
who follow me home.

Glide

After I launched a 1979 Chrysler Newport between threads
of electrical lines and into the neighbor's stone wall,

my dad and I rebuilt it—stone by stone—in two hours
flat, and I quit driving. It was only my third week

on the road alone, and I had totaled the large green car
respectfully called The Tank. No

convincing could lure me back to the wheel, not even
my mom's new Honda. But that winter, my father

took me to an empty parking lot on an early Sunday,
with five inches of untouched snow. He spun the wheel

and lifted his hands, looked over at me as my shoulder
banged up against the window, turned three times

around. The surrounding buildings blurred,
the snow blasted light in the swirl and sun with each

uncontrolled turn. I realized, then, that in the spin,
there was a lesson, dizzy and unobstructed.

I don't remember my father braking. We just slid around
the lot until we stopped, both still breathing.

After Asthma Wakes Me, I Breathe on the Porch

my lungs expand   catch the last gasp   before an exhale

in a lake-like ripple   over the tongue   around the head

the path the way   blood might bloom   in water

the sun tracks itself   behind the beached hills   the moon sucks

most colors   everything   dark blackberries

puncture themselves   with their own thorns   in the violent night

the sun brightens   another hemisphere   on this little planet

all the creatures   awake in the dark   crickets full of hum

oh my own blood   blossoms   in this thick mist of air

Skeleton

to the frame   of marrow   the skull   its case for   the brain inside
those bodies   who gave themselves   to science   bones reassembled
for classroom analysis   fuck, take away   my musculature
carve the mass from it   and there   my awkward spine
rid of its ligaments   my disintegrating hips
let these bones   be your study   of the raised ratios
of length and width   to the weight   built upon such scaffolding
to my children   to their bones   I bore inside me   soft
grey and enlarging   to my suspicious breasts
heredity of cancer   to my dying
mother   to the shifting   self that made a self
within this architecture   to my heart
soft pulsing creature   enveloped in bones

Applied Mathematics

You've put your clothes back on and become quiet,
as if I did something wrong. Love, once multiplied
by the power of two, is now just a discreet view
of your stomach as it's curtained beneath your shirt.

My mother winds wool around a common knot, crossing threads
over and over like the math we make of grief. Grief, the study
of change, what we once loved in physical form, the calculus of none.
My father's ashes, heavier than stone. She does not want them.

And what are the absolutes of love? Why do we incrementally
fade from one another? One day becomes ten months, then
it's years since I've seen you. When you say, "It's like nothing
has changed," I remember us sharing the same bench
in the park, drunk and singing.

Consider the measurements of a bench, the eroding
bolts, and how long it will last before it breaks
under someone's weight. Consider my body
falling to the ground, then picking itself up and pushing
through the day without you.

Nothing Broken

I run my finger across the small of your back
		while you fix the sink. You leap and scream,
hitting your head on the countertop. Once, you hid
		a plastic snake in my sleeping bag before
a camping trip, and I screamed before tackling you
		in the tent. "I love you," you say before
you feed me lasagna, mostly missing my mouth.
		Together, we fry donuts. Together, we swim
out to the middle of the pond
		at night to watch the meteor showers,
your hands grabbing my ass while we tread
		water and laugh. You're always fixing something,
detangling the Christmas lights and unknotting
		my necklaces. While working on your car,
I ask you if I need fixing, too—and you
		say, "I'm afraid so"—then you fix me right there
		on the garage floor. We talk
in code while flossing, and we don't let the cats
		get between us in bed. You insist on grilling
while I chop vegetables inside. You are working
		on gender roles. I am working on the last word,
and how I like to have it. I say, "How about
		next time we fight, I'll let you speak last."
You laugh and laugh, I kick you on the couch.
		When we fight for the sheets in bed, I release
them as proof, as truce. You reach back and pinch
		my nose. "Goodnight," I whisper,
fighting your hand. "Goodnight," you say,
		getting the final word after I fall asleep.

Take the Moon

By now we know the moon is not a pocket for the stars,
nor a hammered silver disk pinned to the torn edge
of atmosphere. It's not an open mouth of damp hope
for all the lonely, and it's not lowering large and full
into a sunset moment like a true Buddha.
No. The moon is just a cheap lamp. Under its light,
I smash a joint in the orange sombrero ashtray
you brought me from San Diego, the only gift
I kept after our fourth and final breakup.
The moon's sunken eyes are simply craters,
not a face of *oh no, you're gone.* I realize now I may
never see you again, the soft haze of cigarette smoke
escaping your coffeed lips into the fog. And since
the moon is not you, oh no, I won't ask it again
for peace. I will admit that sometimes, even when
it's in one of its phases and mostly dark, I can still see
its pointless circular shape skulking behind Earth's rude shadow.

My Drunk Boyfriend Tells Me About the Bridge

"It was 1 a.m., and the fog
squeezed the stars out
of the sky. I walked

from Divisidero Street all
the way across San Francisco,
a pint of Wild Turkey

in my pocket. As I approached
the bridge, I saw the gate
was shut, but I watched

the guards let a dude
with a bike pass through. Yeah,
there really is a manned gate.

So I walked up, and after
a few dumb questions
like *where are you going?*

I told them, real easy,
To walk across,
and you know what?

they called the cops,
who 5150ed me. Psych
ward at S.F. General

is no joke—my roommate
tried to scratch all the skin
off his face. Lesson

being, if you want to
to jump from the Golden
Gate at night, bring a bike."

Ars Etcetera

My dog wakes me at 3 a.m. two
nights in a row to crap
and it's raining as usual. I'm inspired
for a moment by the emptiness
of night, the dark street's dim
glow from porchlights.

I feel more like a poet when
I see the street in those terms.
I wore the wrong shoes to walk
the dog in the rain, my feet are
cold and wet, and that is fact.

Sometimes the mundane
is just mundane, though—not poetry—
and later another unfortunate fact appears,
a possible rip in the story of the day
while I'm on the couch in warm socks,
snoozing through the similes.

I resist writing. Of course I do.
The same faces persist in the news,
stories always troublesome, a wall,
a war, a shot-up bar. It is so cold
in the Midwest that all of the cars
are frozen to the ground. I'm stuck,
too, trying to find my own melt.

My dog is too old for trips to the ocean,
and somehow I'm aging too, despite my
youthful enthusiasm for wine and that year
all of my techno-bubble-Adderall friends
were younger than me. I'm writing these days
so I probably won't go dancing.

The New Yorker magazines pile up
in defeat. My foot twitches uncontrollably.
Just one more minute in bed, and I will
start another day with this poem, a poem
I have no idea what to do with.

Italy Report

I've been in Italy for six days and no tongue,
no ride on a moped behind the broad shoulders
of Alberto with the long hair. Plenty of wine,
as expected, but it's hard to feel drunk here
with all of the sheep. I cup the sheep dog's face
in my hands. The sheep herder calls, *Andiamo*!
and they all take off for the hills. The air smells
like milk, wet sheep shit, and the linden tree.
I can barely sleep. The birds are up at 4:30,
whistling their worm songs. The worms
rise up from their rooms after the rain.
I retreat to think about how to write
an Italy poem without sounding like a lucky-ass
bitch. I feel lucky right now, and you know
what that means? It means we can all have cake
for breakfast. Maybe if we just eat more olives,
everyone will shut their mouths, or open up,
let the giant drops of rain fall fat on their tongues.

The Invitation from my Shower

When I floss my teeth, it's an accomplishment.
I await the invitation from my shower.
I've worn holes though my favorite cat shirt,

but I bought an extra one just in case. I smell bad,
but I like it, kind of like the former lover years ago
who crawled in my bed after closing hour,

and he stunk so good. Deodorant
unapparent, Ramones' covers, cigarettes
and beer sweat. Yesterday,

I watched a man sleep in his Ford SUV
at the 7-Eleven until he woke up and saw me, threw
his lotto tickets out of the window and drove away.

I usually wake up in cat fur. I cradle my laptop
in my bed 'til the happy pills kick in. At night,
I sometimes call my brother, moping about being alone.

To be clear: alone. Not lonely. I told
my friend Jeffrey I live alone with two housecats
and a sink full of dishes all wanting attention.

He compared me to some other ass-kisser who bought him
a cake on his last day of work and he hasn't
called me back. Who needs him? Me. Once

he said I had fortune cookies in my bra and we laughed
and cried. What would be my luck? He would hate
that I miss him even in the drive-thru,
my black jeans covered in cat fur.

Neckhugger

I swipe left for turtlenecks on
Tinder.

Can we all agree that nothing
about them says *come hither*?

The only way to wear one is
up over your nose and mouth,
breathing heavily.

And you wonder why I'm single
and everyone is meeting
at the ski lodge without me.

Smack Talk

Blink and I'm behind
your back, talking crap
about your newest microdrama:
another spider in the tub,
a broken toe, another
abandoning. You are
my little snack, a hook
that snags me. I laugh
at your fat, thick through
the ass, the stack of clothes
you keep under the bed
as if you might bounce back.
I get you and you hate
that fact. You shut me out,
sink into the couch
with your Sauvignon Blanc
and everything flattens, but
don't think I don't see you.
I smell the sloth from your
window. A little metal bean
burrows behind your heart
in a constant state of gunshot.
Blink and I'm behind you,
holding a rat by its tail.
You worry I might come
back, but I've never left,
darling. I'm always right
here with a mirror
and a little slap, something
to get you cracking.

In Vino Veritas

I had a thirst for it. I knew what time
they started to sell it. I barely moved
between my bed and my couch.

When I could think of something else,
I thought about quitting tomorrow,
about dying, about who would take

my cats. After a certain point, the liver
can't heal. After a certain point, you are
everything you've ever done to yourself.

*

Before I left the for the airport, I emptied
the last bottles into the sink, swore
when I got back, no more, no more

shaky hands, the same gray sweats. I was
leaving the city for Kauai: waterfalls,
painted chickens wandering the shoreline.

When I got to the airport, I met
Kelly at the gate. Oh my god, she said,
are you okay, the color of your eyes.

*

Already dark before they checked me in.
Nurses footsteps kept me awake for hours.
I pulled out my hair into a pile. Doctors

said: eighteen pounds of fluid drained
from my abdomen. How much were you
drinking a day? If I lied, they wouldn't know

how to keep me alive. Offered rehab,
I refused. So to confirm, you are refusing
help, a nurse said, shaking her head.

*

At home after six days, my cats cleaned
my hand. I told them I loved them despite
the furniture, couldn't muster as much

for myself. I wanted to move far away
from what happened. I couldn't look
at the body I nearly left. Now, I pray,

let God, if out there in the density
of night, give me grace. Let a person emerge
from the mess, alive with rushing blood.

III.

Full of Grace

Before the funeral service,
my uncle tells me he recently
fell into a large flowerpot,

smashing the poor baby flowers.
Hard not to laugh together.
The church seems smaller

than it ever has,
but then so does God.
I still genuflect, say Hail Mary

for Grandma in Heaven—*full of grace*—
can't help myself, Catholicism
embedded in my active gestures

like a middle finger at a traffic merge.
The statue of Jesus opens
his palms to the sky.

My mother begins to raise her hands
towards the ceiling as if in prayer
but then actually to her nose,

sneezes, says, "It's the incense."
I whisper, "You're allergic to God."
Hard for my uncle not to cry when

we leave the church. A grave
waiting, a canvas canopy shielding
the sun. Again we pray, and I guess

it's time for that, the sky clear
and endless. The children take
the roses from the casket.

Death is new to them, and distant.
My mother reminds me
it was supposed to rain and later

it does, at dusk, as if it had been
waiting for something.
A short burst. We drive past

my grandmother's house once
more and nearby, teenagers
cluster on a stoop. A girl abruptly leaps

into a handstand and, on her palms,
walks down the street, the bright soles
of her sneakers deflecting the water.

Age Report

I step onto the scale while holding my cat,
and the math part of my brain scrambles:
because either he weighs 25 pounds
or I'm the one who gained the weight.
Now, I won't weigh myself
without him. A friend once said,
isn't gaining weight just part of being
in your forties? I'm afraid of the number
of fudge-dipped macaroons I ate in the past
24 hours, but I'm not afraid of much else
anymore, and you can thank my forties for that.
Thanks to my thirties, I relived my twenties,
and thanks to my twenties, I actually lived.
I don't know why I was so depressed
most of the time back then except to say
that I've since realized anxiety
is a freaked-out cat to the overturned turtle
of depression, and there's a pill for both.
I had an abandoned pair of boxers in my bed
kind of problems back then. Don't worry—
I've lost count of the number of years
that I didn't not "fail better," but failing better
does not mean failing more. The ground
just becomes harder to fall against as you
get over a certain threshold—and maybe for you,
that happens in your fifties, but I just had
two bang-up years in and out of the hospital
and I blame failing and falling in my forties.
It just looks messy now, and there's nothing like
like another sleepless night of worry to keep you from
from your true path. But is there really such a thing
as a true path? I'm in my forties and I hope
I didn't miss it! I can't find it, but it could still
be out there. Maybe I'm just not seeing clearly.
It must be my eyes.

Collapsing Plate

—after the film, *Ghost*

I am no Demi Moore and there's no Patrick Swayze kissing my shoulders
or stroking my arms, but as I plant my elbows in my thighs, curve my palms
into a perfect rotating C-cup mound of clay and it centers,
attaches itself to the spinning surface, a slippery mess on my hands,
the clay does what I tell it to like a good little lump.
I open it up, my crisscrossed thumbs pushing down from the center
towards the base. When the clay looks dry, I water it with my sponge
and begin to pull the mouth of the vessel towards me as it turns, stretching
it wide. This will likely be a plate, as mugs are overrated
with their stupid handles. I used to be better at throwing
on the wheel, more patient with my fingers, and I can't pinch much
these days but this clay volcano, looted funeral pyre, this mound
of Venus. I'm okay with it. I'm okay with a lot, it seems,
as the edge of the plate slides through my fingers and joyfully spins,
wobbles, buckles, folds, and exhausted, collapses to the wheel.

At the Gallery

I don't know why I bother.
I'm the one in the corner
who gulps the free rose
and strains to find the stunt
that stirs the biggest riot:
some secret spit
on the rusted urn or
a perfect fist through
the headless bust.

Yet no one dares to roast
the artist, his pallid trust
in friends who fuss over
his "abstracted" rain,
an agonizing burst of stars
above a campfire. I'm probably
the shallow one, too smug
to put my own iron in
the flame, to make my own
unfit decapitations.

Still, there's always
time to stuff an apple
into the mouth of my
hoggish frustrations.

Ice Cream Truck

We will have cones, please.
Vanilla with rainbow sprinkles.
We will have the whole ice cream truck
and the street it is on. One serving
of the fence by the water. The water. We
will take the lamppost, the trees lining
the street, the bridge in the background.
We will take one of each building.
The entire city in the background.
Please serve us, as the sign says.
Sprinkles on everything. Give us
a house in the hills and only good
dogs that don't bark or bite. Cookies
and a cask of merlot. A winery.
We would like to order a king-
sized bed with a side of pillows.
We want something besides
popcorn and popsicles now.
We would not like one of your
popsicles. We have big plans.
Plans to freeze cream on
a satellite. With your funding,
we will have the first ice
cream on Mars. What's our pitch?
We want the shared desire
to serve a specific consumer
need. We want to recreate
the feeling of live bodies in a pile
while listening to Lizzo.
We want the feeling of mommy
hands cradling our heads.

Martha Stewart on the Cover of the Sports Illustrated Swimsuit Issue

Martha Stewart looks hot in her golden shawl

Her blown-out hair fans over her neck, cheeks pink as peonies

She leans into the wooden deck, somewhere tropical probably

Maybe she was Photoshopped, maybe it's plastic surgery

But nothing about her boob line says I'm too old for this

Did you know Martha was once a model

Once she was a model prisoner

A low-security penitentiary, sure

Maybe she was allowed one phone call a day

Maybe she wrote an entire cookbook about canned peas in there

Martha doesn't have much to say about prison anymore

No one wants to make the usual comments about female objectification

No one wants to think about the inner Martha, beneath the swimsuit

We know she likes holiday decorations and Cornish game hens

We know she has great on-screen chemistry with Snoop Dog

We have purchased cloth napkins from her home décor line at Macy's

She is bad with taxes, we definitely know that

But good at making money, and that's nothing to laugh at

Yet Martha as the cover model for Sports Illustrated

I did not see that coming

I spent all day trying to imagine what she might have been thinking

Martha said something about looking and feeling good at any age

People who talk about her age are just scared of their own

But not Martha—she's ready for anything at 81

When I look at her on the magazine cover in her swimsuit

I don't care what some men may think

Whether or not they keep it under their mattress

If I stare long enough at her smile and eyes

I find myself practicing her face, saving it for later

This Great Nation

I believe all Americans should understand their constitutional rights, unless they're stuck in line at the Post Office.

The Post Office is an American institution, just like all of the 4H pony rides in Nebraska.

The state of Nebraska was founded with the guiding principles, don't bellyflop in a plastic pool.

The swimming pools of America are gathering places for fitness and fun, just like your uncle's beer belly.

An epidemic of obesity has overwhelmed this great nation, but everyone has room for one more corn maze.

American farmers feed this nation and others with a personal complex over the cowlicks in their hair.

The ranches of the west raise the world's finest cattle for dancing the two-step on sawdust floor.

Only in America, can you buy fleas in a metal tin.

We the people sleep head to toe in snuggies.

Pokemon, an American minister who collects stuffed hedgehogs.

America, we stand united for allergy free versions of foam core!

America, we weep over roller derby carnage.

Best Audience

Sometimes you just want to talk to someone—
a mime in the stairwell, your diabetic cousin,
the man on the train who groans as he falls back
into the seat as the train lurches onward. You don't ask
if he is okay. Never run on pavement, he says.
You don't have to worry about that, you don't say,
still uninspired by treadmills, still thinking
in patterns, stupid choices on replay. Still complaining
to your coworker about Coke Zero and the latest revolt
on grains. Also, you are scatterbrained and it's not
reversing. Later, you remember you left your
phone on your desk and there's only one person to blame.
There's only one person to blame and you mutter all the way
back to the office, no one to talk to. Then someone offers
you a handful of popcorn, and you're talking to someone
about more butter. You're talking to ducks
the next day by the lake! You see your friend
in the cereal aisle. He says he's doing okay.
You like talking to others when it's too hard to talk
to yourself, when there are only mean things to say.

Resting Pose

Leaning over the pylon and spitting sunflower seeds
into the tributary is not what you'd call productive:
there are no new flowers magically waving

from the riverbanks, and your lawn's not mowed, but it's better
than doing nothing, lying on your back and watching
grass grow—which is what you did yesterday,

which is why you're not mowing it, having noted no progress.
Sometimes progress happens with very little effort: your cousin
stopped speaking to his wife and got the golf vacation

with his buddies from work; your little sister pretended
to hold her breath in the toy store until she got a new doll
that the dog maimed significantly in two minutes flat

after she left it on the couch. Sometimes complacency
can result in having your face chewed off, but sometimes
it can end in contemplation. You've written a few solid lines

moments after you zoned out to the TV on mute.
But poems don't finish themselves, and now you have
a choice—to wrap this one up or continue considering

the fruit flies hovering over the compost pile.
Did you know mayflies are also called "Ephemeroptera"
because they only live fully developed for a few hours, frantic

to make the end of their lives satisfying?

Nothing Cute to See Here

I'm hungry and there is half of a tuna fish sandwich
in my fridge that I probably won't revisit. I have two
cats who seem to be aware of the sandwich since
they've been keeping vigil in the kitchen for the last
hour, but I'm sure you already know enough without
me telling you how cute they are. On the other hand,
my smelly dog was a squirrel enthusiast with one
floppy ear and a spotted tongue. He rarely barked.
He would wait for me in the window. The vet put him
to sleep on the cold linoleum at the emergency clinic.
Did you know they give animals methadone to let
them die easy? You could have given me the same
shot right then—I would have gone down with him.

Wedding Poem

—for Kelly & Robert

After crossing over the flooded stream
and into barren fire road,
after walking through the overgrown shrub
and past coyote scat,
their backpacks crowding their sweaty backs
and holding a weight
not unlike a past
that every person carries with them,
they stop at a crest.

Take a breath.

They look out onto the old ocean
and the whole world is before them,
as close as the coarse brush
that scratches their cuffs
and as far as the hazy line that binds
the sea to the sky.

The sun sutures this certain edge
and yes, here is where they will
put down their packs,
pitch their tent,
the narrow poles tendering
the ground in a soft way.

Here they will strike a fire with the branches
they have gathered. Warm the kettle.

Lean into each other like the tinder
they have built into a little shack.

Burn inside this space.

It's always been this simple:

Keep heat.
Have love.

Too Hot to Happen

Summer throws its door shut,
declares the light must lower
itself in the sky. You lower onto
onto the floor, extend your legs across
the cool linoleum, swirl your ice
around the damp cup of ice water,
your hair damp at the nape. The cats,

too, have surrendered their full bodies
to the floor, fleas popping off
their necks under the veil of stagnant
air. To move would mean you could
handle it, hold a long yoga pose
while sweat drops off your chin
with intention. You've lost the will

to stare at a fixed point while holding
your leg over your shoulder. Lost
the moxie to suck in your gut, get
out there, show a little leg at Dolores
Park. Today will not be the day you
join the gym again or deny your base
cravings. Bring out the Cornettos.

And although it's too hot to cook,
too hot to eat, too hot to move
across the room to the diabetes
commercial on the radio, you let
the ice drop and bump in the damp
glass. Let your thighs stick together
when you trudge across the rug

wearing loose cotton, only cotton.
The birds have gone to bed early,
and you sit with an icepack balanced
on your head. Maryanna knocks
on the screen door with one of the last
summer tomatoes, and you imagine
slicing it in the morning for breakfast.

Sleep Paralysis

The road is dry and also wet. I cannot
find a breath to fill my stiffened lungs nor grasp
something to cure me. It's dark outside.
The sun burns through the last of night.
Last night, I walked a glittering path
to get here, asthmatic. I never arrived. I woke
up not knowing the street. I pressed the softening
sidewalk with my handprint, wrote my name
and date of birth. That dry day, they filled the dead
potholes with cement. Every day after the rain,
it doesn't rain. Fog firms over the cliffs
or rolls over the trees. I was here once
before but I've never been here
breathing. There are footsteps
walking towards and away from me.
I try to trace their path with my ears, a breath,
my new hand. I do not recognize my hand,
which hand, the one hand I wrote this with.

My Father was a Runner

At the dentist's office,
what if the dental assistant
is told to dispose of the plaster
molds of my father's teeth?
He has been gone for 13 years,
his fucked-up teeth
abandoned before the night
guard could be made.
She places them on
the counter, asks herself,
What the hell happened here?
The front two teeth slightly
overlap as if one tooth
is trying to elbow
the other out of the way,
and the remaining teeth
crowd behind them
like they are all in a race:
bodies packed
at the starting line,
waiting for the gun.

Anywhere Anymore

No downtown or sidewalks, no beer served at the bowling alley. No bowling alley. No hand-
holding at the home team game, no road to the top of Mount Tamalpais, no espresso
in the parklet, no glitter on a Tuesday, no bikini wax or leg wax or manicure or hand job.
No decent chewing gum, no single-use stemware, no election propositions, no democrats,
no lawn signs, no detritus of an old Bernie bumper sticker peeling from a Subaru Outback.
No tea in the garden in the park, no tents beneath the freeways, no Sundays with mimosas
and brisket. No sushi. No Wonderwall 1995. No single-use condiments. No bridge spanning
a body of water over which you could safely walk without thinking about jumping. No red
leather on a Wednesday, book club on a Thursday. No LSD in the high school gym and no pot
in the porta-potty. No new construction, no luxury condos. No luxury, no cost of living.
The living eat each supper like it's their last and fall asleep on the bus, the bus that left hours ago.

Precise Coordinates

Late afternoon. The gauzy curtains
bandage the window. I stretch

my one mobile leg from bed.
Buckley, my dog who died four years ago,

sits framed on my dresser, looking at me
from his professional headshot. When we

arrived at the photo studio that day,
the room was alive with the sound

of Chihuahuas squeaking from
their little brains. Still, I couldn't console

his worry. Looking back at me now,
he still appears concerned and I'll take it.

Somewhere beneath the surgical
dressing is my new knee.

Any movement feels as if I'm breaking open
the wound again and again, and I need

to map it, the precise coordinates of my pain.
My entire body wants to curl up and lick itself,

like a dog. They say I should be walking within
a few weeks. I walked Buckley into the clinic

that laid him on the floor to die. Running
barefoot along the Pacific with him,

leaping over the waves. Now, waves of pain pin
my leg to the bed. Heavy and swollen,

the image of my dog softening as the light goes,
his fur still threaded through my old sweater.

Long Season

Can't shake winter this year.
Skipped supper again and still I'm hunched
over my desk as if I'm someone of substance
and determination. If only a cigarette
was hanging out of my mouth, and why not?
A lot has changed: the wine foresworn,
and whatever version of love I hoped for
has lost its wick in the wax.

The trees' leafless branches wobble against
remnants of Pacific wind. Might as well
pull on some jeans and hit the coffee shop,
ask them for a flower in the foam, maybe
summon spring that way. The barista says, "sure"
but I get a fern, foam on my nose.

The fog hovers over the parking lot. But look—
the trees along the curb are showing signs of yellow,
and the bees stir in their winter clusters.
Give me a bulb about to pop through
the muck. A little green wouldn't hurt.
Promise me something is about to grow,
and it better be goddamn beautiful.

Acknowledgements

These poems (often in different versions) appeared in the following journals:

Brain Mill Press: "How I Will Do It"

Cream City Review: "My Father Was a Runner"

The Glacier: "Gorilla," "Applied Mathematics," "Precise Coordinates," "Leaving South of Market"

Global Poemic: "Who Goes to Bars Anymore?"

The Hampden-Sydney Poetry Review: "At the Gallery," "Skeleton"

Home Planet News: "Apology," "Glide," "My Drunk Boyfriend Tells Me About the Bridge"

Miracle Monocle: "Thirteen," "Paresthesia," 'Sleep Paralysis"

New Ohio Review: "Open Mic at Tony's Bar and Grill," "A Working List"

On the Seawall: "Ice Cream Truck"

One Art: "Long Season," "Piece by Piece"

The Pinch: "Swerve"

Pine Hills Review: "The Invitation from My Shower"

Pine Row Press: "Take the Moon"

Rattle: "Weather Report with Turkeys"

San Diego Poetry Annual: "When I Am Cold"

Shrew: "Wish Control," "Obvious Cracks"

The Shore: "Answer the Question," "Best Audience"

SWWIM: "After Asthma Wakes Me, I Breathe Again on the Porch"

West Trestle Review: "Full of Grace"

You Blew It!: A Miracle Monacle Micro-Anthology: "Age Report"

Swerve was written before my mother, Nancy Szmurlo Knapp, passed away in late 2024. This book, and every book, is for her.

Thanks to my brother, Shane, for his love and support.

To Kim Addonizio for her insight, friendship and ongoing encouragement for my work.

To Dorianne Laux, John Hoppenthaler, and Jennifer L. Knox for their kind words on this collection.

To Sarah Heckles for designing the perfect book cover, and 20 years of friendship.

Thanks to Hank Hudepohl for his care in selecting this manuscript, and the hard work of making it a reality.

To Dana Jaye Cadman, RJ Ingram, Annie Hampford, and Kendra Tanacea, who provided critical feedback on earlier iterations of this manuscript.

Thanks to the writers in Kim's Saturday morning workshop, the regulars and those who have passed through: Melinda Clemmons, Kelly Grace Thomas, T.R. Poulson, Julia McConnell, Jocelyn Casey-Whitman, Susan Krane, Patricia Wallace, Cynthia Ventresca—I've learned so much from all of you. Also, thanks to Jane Huffman and her workshop participants for indulging me with these poems.

To Peter Bullen, Flower Conroy, Liz Agans, Jen Santiago, Ben Foss, Jeffrey Martin, Geoff Kuffner, Peter Kline, Brittany Perham, David Roderick, Kelly Voet, Robert Wohlers, Angela Basile, Jessica Conner, Leslie Blanco, Elizabeth Sanderson, Melissa Tuckey, Sarah Strickley, Daniel Nester, Sean Singer, Janis Butler Holm, Mark Halliday, David Dodd Lee, and Joe Millar for their poetry, friendship and community.

For the poetry and friendship of Bob Dickerson, who is rocking out on the astral plane.

About the Author

Tracey Knapp is the author of two poetry collections, *Swerve* (Pine Row Press, 2026) and *Mouth* (42 Miles Press, 2015).

She has received prizes and scholarships from La Romita School of Art in Terni, Italy, the Tin House Writers' Workshop, and the Dorothy Sargent Rosenberg Poetry Fund. Her work has appeared in the *New Ohio Review, The Glacier, SWWIM, ONE ART, Cream City Review, The Pinch*, and elsewhere. She has been nominated for Best of the Net and two Pushcart prizes. Originally from New York's Hudson Valley, Tracey lives in the California Bay Area.

Find her at traceyknapp.com.

www.ingramcontent.com/pod-product-compliance
Lightning Source LLC
LaVergne TN
LVHW051019080826
845145LV00009B/2708

* 9 7 8 1 9 6 3 1 1 0 2 4 1 *